SCHOLASTIC

TRUE OR FALSE

Birds

BY MELVIN AND GILDA BERGER

All birds have feathers. TRUE OR FALSE?

TRUE! Birds are also the only animals with feathers.

Birds have different feathers for different uses. Tail and wing feathers are wide and flat. They push against the air and help birds fly. Feathers next to the skin are small and fluffy. They keep birds warm and dry. Small birds have fewer than 2,000 feathers. Swans and other large birds have about 25,000.

Most birds lose their feathers every year and grow new ones.

All birds can fly. TRUE OR FALSE?

FALSE! Not all birds can fly.

Some birds have wings that are too small or stubby for flying. Others have wings that are too soft or weak. Kiwis, for example, have tiny wings that are hard to see. Instead of flying, kiwis walk or run along the ground on their strong, short legs.

The kiwi's shaggy feathers help it move through thick plants.

All birds build nests in trees. TRUE OR FALSE?

FALSE! Only Some kinds of birds make nests in trees.

Other birds build nests near water, on rocky ledges or cliffs, or on the ground. A nest may be as simple as a few twigs piled up. Or it may be made of grass, leaves, mud, or bits of rope, plastic, or feathers. Storks, for example, build big, deep nests in chimneys so that their young will not fall out.

Storks usually return to the same nest every year.

TRUE! Birds lay from one to twenty eggs at a time.

Birds' eggs are all about the same shape, but they vary in size and color. Nearly all parent birds keep their eggs warm until they hatch. Small birds usually lay small eggs that hatch in about ten days. Large birds typically lay large eggs, which can take more than a month to hatch.

The eggs of the American robin take about twelve to fourteen days to hatch.

Most parent birds care for their young.

TRUE OR FALSE?

TRUE! Parent birds usually feed and protect their babies for weeks.

The baby birds are often born helpless. Their eyes are closed and they cannot see. The newborns have few or no feathers. They're too weak to fly or stand. The parents find food and keep their young safe.

Only a few kinds of birds — chickens, ducks, and swans — can find their own food soon after they are born.

Birds chew
their food.

TRUE
OR
FALSE?

FALSE! Birds don't have teeth.

They use their beaks, or bills, to get food. Then most birds swallow it whole. Birds that eat fish use their long, wide beaks to scoop food from the water. Seed eaters have short, strong beaks that can crack open shells. Birds that eat fruit have sharp, pointed beaks — good for slitting fruit skins.

Birds also use their beaks to build nests and fight enemies.

The peregrine falcon is the fastest bird.

TRUE OR FALSE?

TRUE! No other bird can travel faster than a peregrine falcon.

In fact, a peregrine falcon is faster than any animal on Earth. It often swoops down on its prey at a speed of about 200 miles (321.8 kilometers) per hour. Compare this to the cheetah, the fastest land animal. Its top speed is only approximately 70 miles (112.7 kilometers) per hour.

Birds also breathe faster than any other animal.

The ostrich is the biggest bird.

TRUE OR FALSE?

TRUE! The ostrich holds the record as the world's biggest bird.

Ostriches may be taller than full-grown people and weigh up to 300 pounds (136 kilograms)! But did you know that the ostrich is as strong as it is big? One kick with its powerful leg can knock over an enemy. A slash with a single long, sharp claw can rip its prey apart.

An ostrich can't fly, but it can run 40 miles (64 kilometers) per hour.

The Nuthatch is the smallest bird.

TRUE OR FALSE?

FALSE! The bee hummingbird is the smallest bird in the world.

This extremely small bird is shorter than a human thumb — only 2 inches (5 centimeters) long! Its nest is the size of half a walnut shell. Like other hummingbirds, the bee hummingbird mostly feeds on nectar, a sweet liquid found inside many flowers.

The bee hummingbird lives only in Cuba.

Owls can see in the dark. **TRUE OR FALSE?**

FALSE! Owls cannot see in total darkness – even with their big eyes.

But owls can see very well in dim light. Unlike most other birds, an owl has eyes that face forward on the front of its head. Its eyes are so large that they can't move up or down or to the sides. However, an owl can easily turn its head around to see in almost all directions.

Owls fly without making sounds.

Vultures
eat other
animals.

TRUE
OR
FALSE?

TRUE! Vultures eat animals, but they are not killers.

Vultures feed mostly on the meat of animals that are already dead. These large birds sit in trees or soar overhead, seeking dead animals. Sometimes they fly in circles, waiting for wounded or ill animals to die. The birds use their excellent senses of smell and sight to help them find their prey.

Vultures are cousins to hawks and eagles.

Male birds are usually brighter in color than female birds. TRUE OR FALSE?

TRUE! The males of many bird species have brighter colors to help attract females.

Bright colors on male birds also warn other males to keep away. The male peacock is among the most colorful of all birds. He fans out his very bright back feathers to catch the female's eyes. Sometimes it works — but sometimes she just walks away!

Some male birds even "dance" to show off their colorful feathers to females.

Penguins can fly.

TRUE OR FALSE?

FALSE!

Penguins are good swimmers and divers – but they cannot fly. The penguins' small, stiff wings act as paddles to help them speed through the water. Penguins spend most of their lives in the water, looking for fish to eat. But when it's time to lay their eggs and raise their young, the penguins come onto the land.

Penguins are the only birds that paddle with their wings, not their feet.

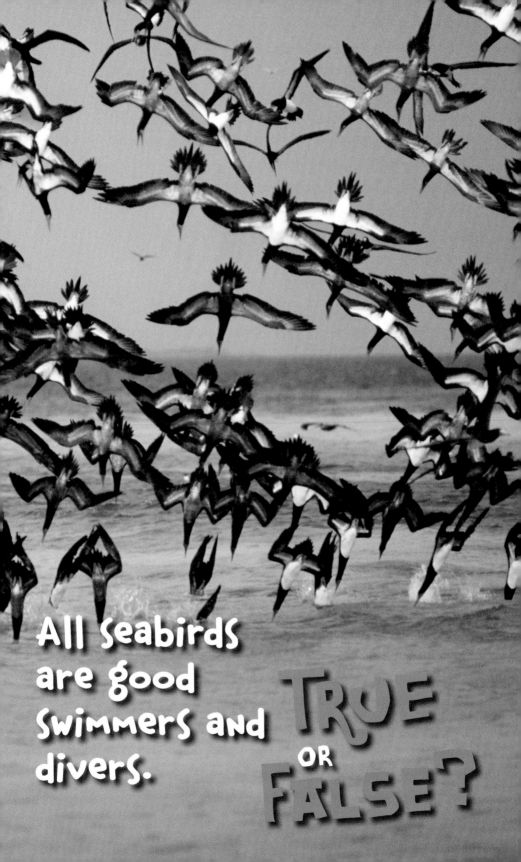

All seabirds are good swimmers and divers. **TRUE** OR **FALSE?**

FALSE! Not all seabirds spend their time swimming and diving.

Some seabirds are simply great flyers. They just skim over the water, looking for prey. Most small petrels and black skimmers feed this way. Some of these birds fly so low that they look like they are walking on water. Occasionally, the birds swoop down and pick up tiny sea creatures in their beaks.

Petrels stay at sea except when nesting.

All birds sing.

TRUE OR FALSE?

FALSE! Fewer than half of all birds sing.

Nearly all the rest have voices, but they don't sing. Many birds make a single sound, or call. Ducks *quack*, for example. Owls *hoot*. Gulls *squeal*. Baby birds *peep* when they are hungry. Many bird sounds carry over long distances. They can even be heard in forests when the birds are hidden.

Pelicans and a few kinds of storks make almost no sounds.

Woodpeckers eat tree bark.

TRUE OR FALSE?

FALSE! woodpeckers make holes in trees to get to their food.

The bird hammers the tree with its beak. Then it pushes its long, sticky tongue into the hole it has made. Any insects it catches make a meal for the woodpecker. Some woodpeckers also eat fruits and nuts, or insects they find on the ground.

A woodpecker's tongue can reach beyond the tip of its long beak.

Some birds change color twice a year. TRUE OR FALSE?

TRUE! A few kinds of birds change color to hide from their enemies.

In winter, some birds, like ptarmigans, have white feathers. This helps them blend in with the snow where they live. In summer, the birds shed their white feathers and grow black- and brown-speckled ones. This helps the ptarmigans blend in with the ground and the plants where they build their nests.

Ptarmigans have short feathers on their feet for walking on snow.

Geese fly
South for
the winter.

TRUE
OR
FALSE?

TRUE! In the fall, many geese travel, or migrate, long distances to warmer places.

Geese fly south because winter is coming. Cold weather freezes the lakes and covers the ground with snow. The geese cannot find the water plants, grasses, or grains they eat. In spring, the snow and ice melt, and plants start to grow. The geese fly back to their northern homes.

Some geese fly nearly 5 miles (8 kilometers) high.

The albatross can fly a year without stopping.

TRUE OR FALSE?

TRUE! The albatross is a long-distance flyer that can go many months without rest.

Huge wings let the albatross glide on the wind for days without flapping. Occasionally, the bird drops down to the sea to seize a fish in its strong beak. The large bird comes to land only to lay eggs and raise its young.

Albatrosses take short naps while flying.

Some birds can talk.

TRUE
OR
FALSE?

TRUE! People can teach certain birds to say a few words.

Talking birds can imitate the human voice. Gray parrots and parakeets are among the best talkers. But some mynah birds can learn to talk better than parrots and parakeets. A number of talking birds can even whistle.

One parakeet learned more than 1,000 words.

Hummingbirds can fly backward.

TRUE OR FALSE?

TRUE! Hummingbirds are the only birds that can fly backward.

These excellent flyers can even fly upside down or hover in one place in the air. They are able to do this because hummingbirds flap their wings more than fifty times a second. While they hover, they use their long, thin beaks to sip nectar.

The giant hummingbird is the largest hummingbird.

Flamingos have webbed feet like ducks.

TRUE OR FALSE?

TRUE! Webbed feet let flamingos walk in soft mud without sinking.

Flamingos use their feet to help them find food in the bodies of water where they live. The birds stir up the mud at the bottom of the water with their feet. Then they stick their heads into the water to catch the tiny plants and animals that they eat.

A flamingo's ankle is halfway up its leg.

Index